HELICOPTERS

A TRUE BOOK

by

Darlene Stille

Children's Press®

A Division of Grolier Publishing

New York London Hong Kong Sydney
Danbury, Connecticut

Reading Consultant
Linda Cornwell
Learning Resource Consultant
Indiana Department of
Education

A swarm of
helicopters

Library of Congress Cataloging-in-Publication Data

Stille, Darlene R.
    Helicopters / by Darlene Stille
        p.   cm. — (A true book)
    Includes index.
    Summary: Briefly describes the way a helicopter operates, different
kinds of choppers, what the pilot does, and some of the work for which
helicopters are used.
    ISBN 0-516-20335-5 (lib.bdg.)   0-516-26171-1 (pbk.)
    1. Helicopters—Juvenile literature. [1. Helicopters.] I. Title. II. Series.
TL716.2.S75 1997
629.133'352—dc20
                                                    96-25729
                                                    CIP
                                                    AC

Contents

This helicopter hovers above a misty forest.

Watch It Fly

A helicopter flies by. It suddenly stops and hangs in the air. It makes so much noise! It sounds like someone chopping wood very fast.

The helicopter flies forward, backward, and even sideways! It can go straight up or down. Unlike an airplane, it does not

A helicopter can land where airplanes cannot.

need a runway to take off or to land.

The helicopter also has no wings. What holds it up in the air?

How Does a Helicopter Fly?

A nickname for helicopter is "whirlybird." That name comes from the big blades it has on top of its body. The blades whirl around, and these whirling blades make the helicopter fly. But how?

Air rushing under the wings keeps this airplane up.

The blades of a helicopter do the same job as an airplane's wings.

An airplane can soar up into the sky because air rushing over and under the wings lifts and holds the plane up.

The helicopter's rotating blades allow it to stay in the air.

As the helicopter blades whirl around, the air rushing over and under the blades lifts the helicopter up.

The helicopter blades are called the rotor. Some rotors have two blades, and others

Helicopter blades are attached to the rotor (left). Some big helicopters, like the one below, have two rotors.

have as many as eight blades. A motor turns the rotor blades.

Some helicopters have a long tail sticking out from the body. A small rotor on the end of the tail helps the pilot steer the helicopter.

Other helicopters do not have a tail. Instead, they have two big blades on each end of the body. The blades whirl in opposite directions, and this controls how the helicopter moves.

Big and Small Helicopters

Helicopters come in all sizes. The smallest helicopters carry only one or two people. The people sit in a glass bubble.

Small helicopters have landing gear that looks like skis. They have one main rotor and a long tail with a small rotor.

The insides of some medium-sized helicopters look like the insides of vans or buses. They have seats for carrying passengers. After the passengers board, they must fasten their seat belts.

Some helicopters are huge. These helicopters can carry either passengers or freight. The biggest helicopters can carry cars or trucks.

Governments use big helicopters to carry soldiers and officials. The president of the United States flies short distances in a special big helicopter.

The president doesn't need a car, he has a helicopter!

Some big helicopters have two rotors. They can have one rotor above the other, or one rotor in front and one in back. Big helicopters also have wheels.

But whether they are big or small, helicopters cannot fly very fast or go very far. They burn fuel too quickly to travel great distances.

What the Pilot Does

The helicopter pilot climbs into the cockpit. The cockpit contains the helicopter's controls. There are three basic controls— a lever, a stick, and pedals.

The lever is next to the pilot on the left. Pulling or pushing the lever makes the helicopter go up or down.

The stick is between the pilot's knees. The stick makes the helicopter fly forward, backward, or sideways.

The pedals control the rudder. There are two big rudder pedals on the floor that the pilot steps on to make the helicopter turn.

Cables and rods connect the controls to the rotor blades. They tilt the blades to make the helicopter go up, down, and sideways.

The pilot uses many controls
to fly the helicopter.

It's time to take off! The
pilot's left hand lifts the lever
up, and up goes the helicopter.

The pilot's right hand pulls the stick backward, and the helicopter flies backward. The pilot moves the stick sideways, and the helicopter flies sideways. The pilot pushes the stick forward, and the helicopter flies forward.

Now the pilot pushes on the left rudder pedal to make the helicopter turn left. Stepping on the right rudder pedal makes the helicopter turn right.

This pilot grips the stick
in his right hand and holds
the lever in his left hand.

The pilot decides it is time to land. The helicopter hovers, or stays still in the air, over a building. The pilot wants to land on the roof. There is a clear place on the roof, called the helicopter pad, made especially for landing helicopters.

The pilot's left hand pushes the lever down, and the helicopter goes down slowly. It settles safely on the heli-copter pad. The ride is over.

To the Rescue

Helicopters are often used to rescue people.

Fire departments have used helicopters to transport people from the roofs of burning buildings.

Helicopters can pull people out of water. They can rescue people from a sinking ship or

This helicopter is saving a sailor from a burning ship.

from the raging waters of a flood. The rescuers lower a rope ladder or a seat called a sling. The people climb up the ladder or sit in the sling. Then the helicopter lifts the people away from danger.

Rescuers in a helicopter can save badly injured people on mountains or in swamps where there are no roads. These helicopters are flying ambulances. They can go much faster than an

Helicopters can land in most kinds of terrain to save lives.

ambulance on the street. They carry the injured person to a hospital that has a helicopter pad on the roof.

Flying ambulances carry a full rescue team.

Helicopters can reach the scene of almost any type of disaster. An earthquake or a hurricane can cause damage that blocks the roads so that cars and trucks cannot get in or out. But rescue helicopters fly over the blocked roads and bring in supplies, such as food, water, and medicine. They also fly in doctors and nurses.

Helicopters

The U.S. Army and Navy first used large numbers of helicopters during the Korean War (1950–1953). They transported wounded soldiers to hospitals.

During the Vietnam War (1965–1973), thousands of helicopters were used to carry out many different tasks. Helicopters transported soldiers and supplies, attacked enemy positions, and moved wounded soldiers to hospitals.

In the Persian Gulf War (1990–1991), helicopters moved supplies and destroyed enemy tanks and bases.

Helicopters at Work

Helicopters do all kinds of work.

Radio and television reporters fly in helicopters to cover news stories. They fly over highways to give live traffic reports.

Police use helicopters to track suspects, and some

Farmers in helicopters
spray their fields.

farmers use helicopters to spray
their fields to kill destructive
bugs. Even movie-makers put
cameras in helicopters to film
action scenes in the air or on
the ground.

The helicopter at the right helps a worker install a giant light. Below, a helicopter brings workers to an oil rig in the ocean.

Helicopters are very useful in construction work. They can carry heavy equipment to the tops of buildings or lift metal towers for electric power lines. These helicopters are called flying cranes.

Helicopters take workers to and from their jobs when these jobs are in odd places. Helicopters carry oil workers to drilling platforms in the ocean and lumberjacks to far-away forests.

The First Helicopters

People dreamed of helicopters long ago. The Chinese wrote about this kind of flying machine more than a thousand years ago. They called it a "flying top." They imagined its rotors were feathers. But they did not know how to build one.

An Italian artist named Leonardo da Vinci drew the first pictures of a helicopter more than five hundred years ago. Still, no one knew how to build a helicopter.

35

The first real helicopters were built in France, and the first helicopter flights were made in 1907.

An early French helicopter

Igor Sikorsky in his helicopter

The first practical helicopter was built by a Russian named Igor I. Sikorsky. He flew this helicopter in the United States in 1939.

Part Plane, Part Helicopter

There is one type of aircraft that is like a helicopter but also like a plane. It is called a V/STOL. This stands for Vertical Short Take-Off and Landing.

A V/STOL has the best features of helicopters and airplanes. When it is in the air, it can fly like a plane because it has wings and engines like a plane. But the engines can be turned to make the V/STOL go straight up or down—just like a helicopter.

They can be turned to make the V/STOL fly forward. V/STOLs might one day be used to carry passengers for small airlines. They could carry people to and from places that do not have large airports.

Tomorrow, A Family Helicopter?

Today, some inventors dream about making small helicopters that everyone could own, just as they own a car. People with private helicopters could fly over traffic jams. They could fly across lakes, and around

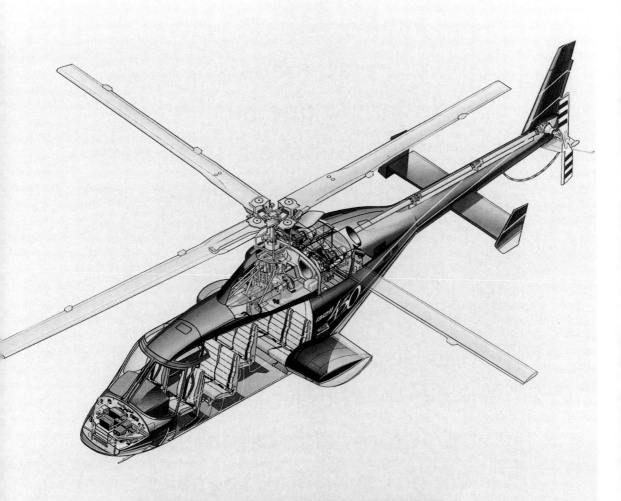

Will a helicopter like this one
replace the automobile?

mountains, and go where there are no roads.

So far, no one has figured out how to make a small, safe helicopter that families could afford.

But people dreamed of helicopters long before any-one discovered how to build them. And maybe someday in the future, another inventor will discover how to make today's dream of the family helicopter come true.

To Find Out More

Here are some additional sources to help you learn more about helicopters:

 **Books**

 **Organizations**

Baker, David. **Helicopters.** Rourke, 1987.

Maynard, Christopher. **Helicopters.** Kingfisher, 1993.

Nielsen, Nancy J. **Helicopter Pilots.** Macmillan, 1988.

Scarborough, Kate. **Why It Goes: Helicopters.** Barron, 1994.

Helicopter Association International
1635 Prince Street
Alexandria, VA 22314

Helicopter Club of America
c/o American Helicopter Society
217 N. Washington Street
Alexandria, VA 22314

Whirly-Girls (International Women Helicopter Pilots)
P.O. Box 7446
Menlo Park, CA 94026

Online Sites

Army Equipment Photo Gallery
http://www.jmu.edu/rotc/gallery.html

Site containing numerous photographs of army helicopters.

Aviation Digest
http://www.avdigest.com

Central site for aircraft enthusiasts has hundreds of links to other aircraft-related sites.

National Air and Space Museum
http://www.nasm.edu

Home page of the Smithsonian museum for aircraft.

Important Words

lever control used by the pilot to make the helicopter go up or down

pedals controls used by the pilot to make the helicopter rotate right or left

pilot person trained to fly a helicopter

propellor part of the helicopter that spins and allows the helicopter to fly

rotor the propellor part of the helicopter where the blades are attached

sling special seat used by rescuers in a helicopter to pick someone up

stick control used by the pilot to make the helicopter go forward or backward

V/STOL special aircraft with moving engines that allow it to fly up or down like a helicopter and forward like an airplane.

Index

Meet the Author

Darlene Stille resides in Chicago and is executive editor of the World Book Annuals. She has written several Children's Press books, including *Extraordinary Women Scientists, Extraordinary Women of Medicine,* and four other True Books on transportation.